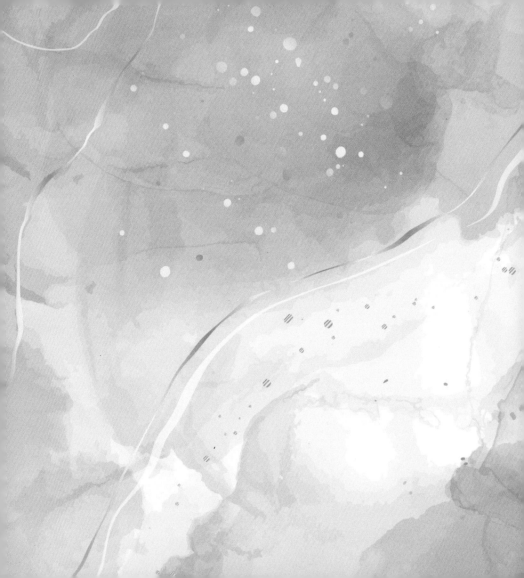

TAYLOR SWIFT

Be Fearless

Keepsake Gift Book

A Gift For:

_____

From:

_____

No matter what happens in life, be good to people. Being good to people is a wonderful legacy to leave behind.

—**Taylor Swift**

Taylor Swift, 2019 iHeartRadio Jingle Ball.

When you hear people making hateful comments, stand up to them. Point out what a waste it is to hate, and you could open their eyes.

—Taylor Swift

I think the first thing you should know is that nobody in country music "made it" the same way. It's all different. There's no blueprint for success, and sometimes you just have to work at it.

—**Taylor Swift**

We don't need to share the same opinions as others, but we need to be respectful.

—**Taylor Swift**

Taylor Swift, 2019 *Billboard* Women in Music event.

My parents taught me never to judge others based on whom they love, what color their skin is, or their religion.

—**Taylor Swift**

I think fearless is having fears but jumping anyway.

—Taylor Swift

Taylor Swift, 2009 concert in Rio de Janeiro.

You are the only one who gets to decide

what you will be remembered for.

—Taylor Swift

Taylor Swift, 2024 concert in London.

I don't think you should wait. I think you should speak now.

—Taylor Swift

In my opinion, the only way to conquer stage fright is to go up onstage and play. Every time you play another show, it gets better and better.

—**Taylor Swift**

Anytime someone tells me I can't do something, I want to do it more.

—**Taylor Swift**

Taylor Swift, 2013 Victoria's Secret Fashion Show.

Red is such an interesting color to correlate with emotion, because it's on both ends of the spectrum. On one end you have happiness, falling in love, infatuation with someone, passion, all that. On the other end, you've got obsession, jealousy, danger, fear, anger, and frustration.

—**Taylor Swift**

The Reputation Stadium Tour, Wembley, London (2018).

Words can break someone into a million pieces, but they can also put them back together.

—**Taylor Swift**

I've had every part of my life dissected . . . When you live your life under that kind of scrutiny, you can either let it break you, or you can get really good at dodging punches.

—**Taylor Swift**

I've always felt music is the only way to give an instantaneous moment the feel of slow motion. To romanticize it and glorify it and give it a soundtrack and rhythm.

—**Taylor Swift**

Taylor Swift, 2014 Victoria's Secret Fashion Show.

I have this really high priority of happiness and finding something to be happy about.

—**Taylor Swift**

Grow a backbone, trust your gut, and know when to strike back. Be like a snake—only bite if someone steps on you.

—Taylor Swift

At some point, you grow out of being attracted to that flame that burns you over and over again.

—**Taylor Swift**

Taylor Swift, 2009 concert in New York City.

I very oftentimes remark that my life is like a fishbowl, and that, like, if I were to . . . fall in love, you know, somebody's choosing to be in that fishbowl with me. To jump into the fishbowl with me and live in that world just with me.

—**Taylor Swift**

Getting a great idea with songwriting is a lot like love. You don't know why this one is different, but it is. You don't know why this one is better, but it is. It sticks in your head, and you can't stop thinking about it.

—Taylor Swift

Taylor Swift, 2019 American Music Awards.

Everybody has that point in their life where you hit a crossroads and you've had a bunch of bad days and there's different ways you can deal with it, and the way I dealt with it was I just turned completely to music.

—**Taylor Swift**

Taylor Swift, 2012 MTV Video Music Awards.

There's something about the complete and total uncertainty about life that causes endless anxiety, but there's another part that causes a release of all the pressures that you used to feel.

—**Taylor Swift**

Taylor Swift, 2019 iHeartRadio Jingle Ball.

Anything you put your mind to and add your imagination into can make your life a lot better and a lot more fun.

—**Taylor Swift**

Taylor Swift, 2015 concert in Toronto.

The lesson I've learned the most often in life is that you're always going to know more in the future than you know now.

—**Taylor Swift**

Taylor Swift, 2016 Grammy Awards.

Everybody has feelings and wants to be seen and loved.

—Taylor Swift

Taylor Swift, 2024 concert in Liverpool.

[*The Tortured Poets Department*] is an album—I think more than any of my albums that I've ever made—I needed to make it. It was really a lifeline for me. Just the things I was going through and the things I was writing about. It kind of reminded me of why songwriting was something that actually gets me through my life.

—Taylor Swift

I've come to a realization that I need to be able to forgive myself for making the wrong choice, trusting the wrong person, or figuratively falling on my face in front of everyone. Step into the daylight and let it go.

—**Taylor Swift**

Taylor Swift, 2012 Grammy Awards.

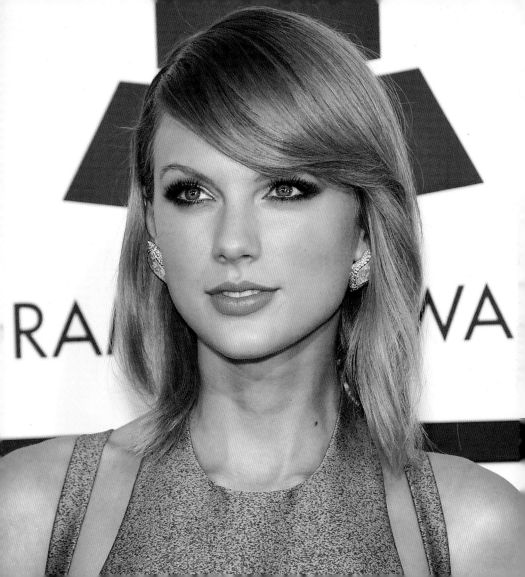

This book is an independent and unauthorized publication. No endorsement or sponsorship by—and no affiliation with—Taylor Swift, *Reputation Stadium Tour*, or any of the companies that offer authorized products and services relating to Taylor Swift are claimed or suggested. All references in this publication to intellectual property owned by Taylor Swift and her affiliated companies are for the purpose of identification, commentary, criticism, and discussion. Purchasers of this book are encouraged to buy the authorized products and services related to Taylor Swift.

Images from Shutterstock.com: Brian Friedman (Cover, 3, 48-49); Melinda Nagy (5); SueST (7); Tinseltown (9, 45, 56); Featureflash Photo Agency (11); RawPixel.com (13); A.PAES (14-15, 29); Andrey Muravin (19); Everett Collection (21, 38-39); FashionStock.com (23, 31); Paul Cotney (25); Christian Bertrand (26-27); Anna Kraynova (29); Kathy Hutchins (33); Iuliia Tarabanova (35); Andrekart Photography (41); SvedOliver (47); johnpluto (57); Garsya (61); DFree (63).

Images from Alamy.com: PA Images (17, 37); Image Press Agency (43); ZUMA Press, Inc. (51); Thomas Jackson (58-59).

This book is an independent and unauthorized publication. No endorsement or sponsorship by—and no affiliation with—Taylor Swift or any of the companies that offer authorized products and services relating to Taylor Swift are claimed or suggested. All references in this publication to intellectual property owned by Taylor Swift and her affiliated companies are for the purpose of identification, commentary, criticism, and discussion. Purchasers of this book are encouraged to buy the authorized products and services related to Taylor Swift.

ISBN 978-1-4971-0557-7

The Cataloging-in-Publication Data is on file with the Library of Congress.

To learn more about the other great books from Fox Chapel Publishing, or to find a retailer near you, call toll-free 800-457-9112, or visit us at www.FoxChapelPublishing.com.

You can also send mail to:
903 Square Street
Mount Joy, PA 17552

We are always looking for talented authors. To submit an idea, please send a brief inquiry to acquisitions@foxchapelpublishing.com.

Printed in China

First printing